PRAGUE

Editions KINA ITALIA

Introduction

During the second half of the 6th century AD, a number of Slavic tribes settled in the Moldau valley and founded the villages from which Prague would later emerge. Around the 7th century, the Przemyslid tribe prevailed, creating a dynasty that would rule the region for four hundred years.

Between the 9th and 10th centuries, the Przemyslid built two fortifications: Prague Castle and the citadel of Vyserhad. During this epoch, Christianity spread rapidly through the region, preached by saints Cyril and Methodius and promoted by the first Przemyslid prince, Borivoj, and his successors, by erecting within the castle walls a church consecrated to the Virgin Mary, the St. George basilica (905) and the St. Vitus rotunda (925), where the chapel dedicated to

Wenceslas would be built, named after the princely saint who was assassinated by his brother Boleslav in 935. In Prague, a bishopric since 973, the ties between religion and politics became increasingly close. In 1039, an edict by Bretislav I required his subjects to convert to Christianity. In 1085, Henry IV, the Holy Roman Emperor, to whom Bohemia had been a vassal since the 10th century, recognized the sovereignty of Vratislav II, who came to the throne in 1061. In the 12th century, trade and the economy flourished, as did Romanesque art.

Around 1170, the first stone bridge in the city, the Judith Bridge, was completed, connecting the two banks of the Moldau, and in 1257 Ottokar II granted a town charter to the settlements on the left bank of the river, renaming them Lesser Town (Malá Strana), across from Old Town on the right bank, which did not become the capital of the realm until 1287. In 1278, Wenceslas II, who had succeeded Ottokar II, was defeated by Rudolf of Hapsburg at the battle of Marchfeld, and Ottokar's territory was thus reduced to Bohemia and Moravia. In 1305, Wenceslas III, the last Przemyslid king, ascended the throne, but was assassinated a year later. The marriage of his daughter Elizabeth and John of Luxembourg, the king of Bohemia, produced Charles, who was crowned Charles I in 1346 and Charles IV, Holy Roman Emperor, in 1355. His reign (1346-1378) marked an epoch of great splendor for Prague, which became an imperial residence, and in 1338 was given its own town hall. The castle was rebuilt, construction of the St. Vitus Cathedral began, the Charles Bridge was erected, Prague became an archbishopric, numerous convents were built, and the first German university besides the Karolinum college, arose in the new quarter, New Town. In his Golden Bull of 1356, Charles IV sanctioned the independence of the Czech realm from the Empire and gave the king of Bohemia the title of first lay elector of the Empire.

Under Wenceslas IV, who succeeded his father in 1378, Prague, which was now no longer the seat of the imperial residence and in 1389 had led a revolt against the Jews, who were accused of bringing the plague to the city, entered a period of violent social disorder of a religious nature. Receptive to the exhortations of Jan Hus, who denounced the corruption of the church, the people sided with him, and at first he was even supported by Wenceslas himself. After his excommunication (1412), Hus was forced to leave the city, but to reaffirm his ideals, he appeared before the Council of Constance, where he was imprisoned and condemned to burn at the stake for heresy. His execution in 1415 made Hus a national hero.

The already precarious situation, aggravated by Sigismund's ascent to the throne, worsened in 1419 when citizens assaulted the town hall of New Town and defenestrated two Catholic advisors. It was the beginning of the Hussite wars, which involved not only the struggle against the emperor's Catholic forces, but also internal conflicts within the Hussites themselves, who were divided into moderates (Utraquists) and radicals (Taborists), and in the end were defeated in the battle of Lipany in 1434, when Sigismund was recognized by the moderates. In 1448, Prague was occupied by the Utraquist troops of George of Podiebrad, who, excommunicated by the Church, reigned from 1458 to 1471. With the first Hussite king of Bohemia, the city experienced another period of grandeur that continued with George's successor Wladyslaw II Jagiello, even though bitter religious revolts continued. In 1516, Louis Jagiello ascended the throne, but died in the battle of Mohács (1526), leaving the crown of Bohemia to the Hapsburgs. Under Hapsburg domination, Prague once again became the imperial seat and played a preeminent political role, becoming the center of an extraordinary artistic and cultural renaissance that nevertheless conflicted with the Catholic absolutism of the Hapsburgs. In 1618, the defenestration of two Catholic officials from the castle halls marked the beginning of the Thirty Years' War. The rout of White

Mountain in 1620 was the final defeat for the Hussites, and resulted in Bohemia losing all its political and religious privileges. In 1648, the Peace of Westphalia reiterated the absolute predominance of the Hapsburgs over Bohemia.

After a period of prosperity and relative peace, in 1848 simmering Czech nationalism, which took shape in the Reform movement that played a fundamental role in the cultural area as well, exploded in a popular revolt that led to the recognition of some fundamental rights.

With the armistice of 1918, Czechoslovakia became an independent republic headed by Tomás Masaryk. His successor Edvard Benesz entered into an alliance with the Soviet Union in 1935, but in 1938, after the ratification of the Munich Agreement, which annexed a large part of the country to Nazi Germany, he fled to London, where he organized the resistance. In 1945 Prague revolted and welcomed the return of Benesz and the Red Army. Three years later, when Klement Gottwald and the communist party came to power, the nation entered the Stalinist period. In 1968 Alexander Dubcek, the first secretary of the socialist Republic of Czechoslovakia, initiated a series of reforms known as the Prague Spring, which was harshly suppressed by Warsaw Pact troops that occupied the city.

Beginning from the 1977 birth of the Charta 99 civil rights manifesto during the tenure of Gustav Husák, the movement for liberty gradually began to grow. In November 1989, Prague citizens revolted peacefully and elected Václev Havel as president. When Soviet occupation troops left and all civil and political rights were recognized, Czechoslovakia was divided into two separate countries, and in 1993 Prague became the capital of the new independent Czech Republic.

MAP OF THE TOWN

1. Strahov Monastery
2. Loreto Sanctuary
3. The Roses Garden
4. Prague Castle and St. Vitus Cathedral
5. St. Nicholas Church
6. The Baby Jesus Church in Prague
7. The Royal Summer Palace
8. Hanavsky Pavilion
9. Artist's House
10. Synagogue
11. Saint Agnes Convent
12. Charles Bridge
13. Old Town's Town Hall
14. Týn Church
15. Powder Tower
16. People's House
17. Karolinum
18. Tyl Theater
19. Bethlehem Chapel
20. National Theater
21. New Town Hall
22. National Museum
23. Emauzy Monastery

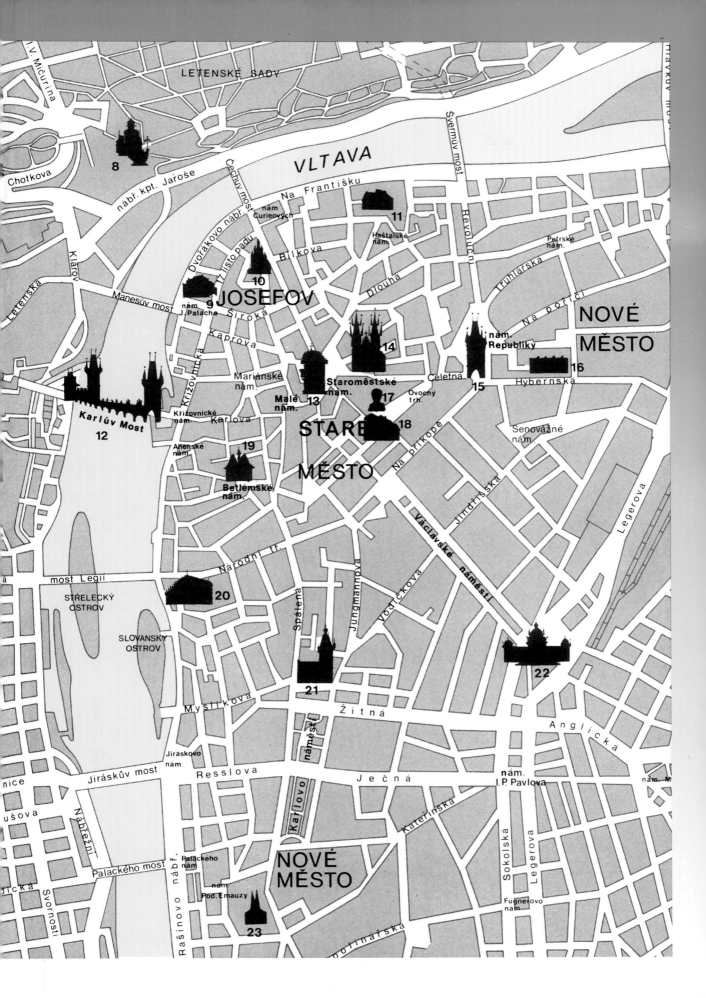

To rediscover the historic roots of Prague, we need to begin right here, in the magical Staré Město, Old Town, the heart of the city we know today. And to follow its development and history, we need to begin at the famous square around which this picturesque quarter grew over the centuries, with its narrow streets and broad roads lined with important monuments, traditional shops, cafés and restaurants: Staromestské Náměstí.

The first merchant communities arose around this Old Town Square between the 10th and 11th centuries, giving the quarter a character that would remain unchanged for many years. The site of the city's largest market during the reign of Sobeslav I (1125-1140), in the 12th century Staré Město became the most important quarter of the city due to the arrival of new communities of merchants from all over Europe, who were responsible for the flowering of public buildings, palaces and monuments. With the ascent to the throne of Wenceslas I (1230-1253), Old Town received a town charter, but not until a century later, in 1338, was it permitted to build its town hall, which was erected on the square. Thus, the future Staromestské Náměstí assumed a leading political role in the history of Prague.

An authentic open-air museum of Prague history and architecture, the southeast corner of the square is dominated by the imposing Týn Church (Tynsky Chrám), second in importance only to the St. Vitus Cathedral. Construction on the church began in 1365, on the site of an earlier primiti-

Above:
Liberty sculpture to Jan Hus.
On the right-hand page:
view of the Old Town Square with the Town Hall Tower.

ve Gothic church from 1270, but it was not completed until the second half of the 15th century. From the beginning, Tyn Church, which stood near Týn Court (Ungelt), the area occupied by foreign merchants since the 11th century, was one of the principal places for spreading the ideas of Jan Hus' reform movement, and it was the leading Hussite church for almost three centuries, at the same time assuming an important symbolic political value as well. Excommunicated by the Church, the Utraquist George of Podiebrad, who reigned as the first Hussite king of Bohemia from 1458 to 1471, decided to attend church right here, after occupying the city with his troops in 1448. The defeat of the Czech rebels in the 1621 Battle of White Mountain and the new imposition of Catholicism resulted in radical changes in the church. Dedicated to the Virgin Mary, the interior of the building was completely remodeled in baroque style, which can clearly be seen in the paintings and sculptures alongside the original works (at the end of the south aisle we can admire the oldest baptistery in Prague, from 1414). The original gold chalice, a symbol of the Hussite faith, which adorned the outside of the church, was also removed and melted down for the gold needed to complete the beautiful statue of the Virgin that replaced it on the pediment. The famous astronomer Tycho Brahe is also buried in the church, now St. Mary of Týn.

In front of the church, a group of beautiful structures built in different epochs (House at Týn, 15th century; House at the White Unicorn, 18th century; and House at the Stone Bell, of medieval origins, with its splendid Gothic style façade) precedes the magnificent Goltz Kinsky rococo palace, built in the second half of the 18th century, with its elegant facade decorated with refined stucco work and allegorical statues of the four elements.

In front of the building, the imposing bronze monument to Jan Hus done

by the Czech sculptor Ladislav Saloun in the early 20th century, was unveiled on the five hundredth anniversary of Hus' death (he was burned at the stake for heresy in 1415, and he later became a symbol of national unity). The majestic figure of the hero dominates the groups of statues below it, which the artist used to summarize the history of the Hussites. Marked first by victory and then by exile, there is also a symbol of hope for the future of the Czech nation, represented by a mother with her child. Of special significance is the fact that in 1918, just three years after the monument was unveiled, the nearby Marian Column was demolished after standing on the square for three centuries as a reminder of the primacy of Hapsburg Catholicism.

The buildings standing on the northeast side of the square were built between the late 19th and early 20th centuries, on the site of earlier buildings that were demolished during restoration of the old Jewish quarter, which once stood right behind this side of the square. During restoration, hundreds of houses and buildings were razed to the ground, resulting in a radical reorganization of the entire quarter and surrounding areas. The most interesting building is the one that now houses the offices of the Ministry of Economy; built in the late 19th century, it is

View of the Liberty sculpture by Ladislav Saloun, devoted to Jan Hus. View of the square.

decorated with a splendid Art Nouveau facade. The building on its right, of 17th century origins, once held a Pauline convent, while the one on its left, built in the early 20th century, is a beautiful example of neo-baroque architecture.

The northwest corner is occupied by the magnificent St. Nicholas Church (Sv. Mikuláš), one of the oldest and historically most important churches in the city. It dates back to the 13th century, when the community of German merchants, who had settled where the Old Town Square stands today as early as the 12th century, built a large Gothic style church consecrated to St. Nicholas, the patron saint of commerce. The church was remodeled a number of times until the first half of the 18th century, when, between 1732 and 1737, it was entirely rebuilt in baroque style by Kilian Ignaz Dientzenhofer.

Assigned to the Benedictine monastery in the 17th century and now a basilica of the Czech Hussite church, throughout its history, the imposing structure played an important role in the secular world as well. In the 13th century, when Old Town did not yet have its own city hall, it served as the seat of local government. After 1785, when Joseph II (1780-1790) suppressed monastic orders, it was used as an archive and then a concert hall.

Views of Old Town Square with St. Mary of Týn Church and the monument devoted to the reformer Jan Hus.

The exterior, dominated by two twin towers that magnificently frame the central cupola, is richly adorned by elegant decorations and beautiful statues, which perfectly set off the complex architectural forms of the church. No less priceless are the paintings by the German Peter Asam the Elder, including the fresco with the Stories of St. Nicholas and scenes from the Old Testament that adorn the cupola. The west side of the square, almost always occupied by the colorful stands of souvenir sellers and picturesque tourist carts, ends at the southern corner with the tower of Old Town's Town Hall (Staroměstská Radnice). The Old Town Hall, which boasts the famous clock, an obligatory destination for anyone visiting Prague, is comprised of various edifices built in different epochs and styles, beginning with the tower and continuing to the 17th century House at the Minute (dům U minuty), famous for its splendid facade entirely decorated with graffiti of mythological subjects and for having been the home of the Kafka family.

In 1338, having obtained from John of Luxembourg the right to build its own town hall, the city chose the already existing house of Wolfin of Kamen (Wolfinuv dům), on the corner of the square, as the site of the municipal building. Thirty years later, the house was expanded with the addition of the present-day tower, which Peter Parler then enlarged in 1381, adding the corner chapel with its bow window with five elegant panes and splendidly decorated interior. In 1410, the famous astronomical clock was placed in the lower part of the tower (the elegant Gothic gate

Above: aerial view of the Old Town Square.

Below: The Old Town Square is always animated by different stands and by picturesque open-air exhibitions.

On the facing page: Town Hall Tower and entrance to the square.

On pages 16-17. Details of the Town Hall Tower: the astronomical clock.

On the left-hand page:
17th century house at the Minute (dům U Minuty) decorated with graffiti of mythological subjects.

On this page: typical house signs.

leads to the stairs that ascend to the panoramic balcony), and had been refined numerous times by 1590. In accordance with theories of the period, the dial depicts the earth at the center of the universe, surrounded by other planets revolving around it. From 8 to 21, when each hour strikes, the sophisticated clock mechanism is triggered and moves the figure of Death (on the right side of the dial). When he turns over his hourglass, a symbol of life slipping by, and pulls the cord that he holds in his right hand, the two small windows above the clock open, and the procession of apostles led by St. Peter begins. When the procession is over, the little windows close and the rooster above crows to end the show. In addition to the figure of Death, the sides of the dial have three other figures that move as the hours strike: the Turk, Vanity and Greed. Below the clock is a calendar with the signs of the Zodiac (19th century).

Over the centuries, the tower has been joined by other Town Hall buildings, including the Kriz House (Krizuv dům), adorned with a splendid grating surmounted by the city's coat of arms, with the motto "Praga caput regni" and the refined window of the 16th century council hall, the Mikes House (dům Mikešů), and the medieval House at the Rooster (dům U kohouta).

Across from the Town Hall, along the south side of the square between Celetná Street and Zelezná Street, are a series of houses and palaces in Romanesque and Gothic style, with picturesque names. The Storch House, built in the 19th century on

On this page, from above:
St. Nicholas Church
Old Town shop
The market

On the facing page: the facade of "U Rotta" House in neo-Renaissance style.

On pages 22-23: The picturesque Melantrichova Lane and Clam Galals Palace.

an earlier Gothic edifice, has a facade decorated with a 19th century painting of St. Wenceslas on horseback; the stone House of the Ram has a frieze above the lovely 16th century gate depicting a ram with just one horn, similar to a unicorn. Following are the House at the Stone Table, built in the 14th century, the House of the Unhappy Poor Man, with Romanesque era foundations, and the 12th century House at the Golden Unicorn. Past Zelezná Street is a group of buildings with gates below them (houses at the Swan, the Red Fox, and the Blue Star), joined to the fifteenth century Ochs House by the narrow Melantrichova Lane, which leads to a pretty little street in the Old Town.

When we finish our visit of the square, we can go on past the Týn Church to the beautiful 14th century Church of St. Jacob (Sv. Jakub). The present baroque style is due to the reconstruction of the building in 1689, which was necessary after the terrible fire that devastated the original church. The interior, adorned with rich stucco decoration, sculptures and paintings, also holds the precious sculpted tomb of Count Wratislav of Mitrovice (1714-1716).

From the Church of St. Jacob, we soon come to the Powder Tower, built in 1475 in honor of Wladyslaw II Jagiello, but completed only in the second half of the 19th century. Near the Tower is the most famous Art Nouveau palace in Prague, the Municipal House (Obecní dům), built between 1895 and 1911 by Antonín Balsánek on the site of the old royal palace, which was demolished in the early 20th century, and recognizable by the large mosaic by Karel Spillar that decorates the facade. In a singular decision, the interior was entrusted to another architect, Osvald Polívka, the famous Czech representative of Art Nouveau, who worked with the leading Czech artists of the epoch, including Alfons Mucha, of course, who is responsible for the splendid painting that adorns the roof of the Mayor's Salon, one of

On the left: Stavovské Theater.

On pages 26-27: view of the square with details of the Ministry of Economy building.

the finest areas of the palace, along with the Smetana Concert Hall, the famous concert hall used by the Prague Philharmonic. On the first floor of the House, the hall is decorated with statues and has a most elegant glass cupola.

Going past the Powder Tower, we come to the old Celetná Street, which along with Karlova Street (which connects the Old Town Square to the Charles Bridge) forms the so-called Royal Mile, the road that Bohemian kings used to travel to the St. Vitus Cathedral for coronation ceremonies. Along the entire road, which is very commercial, are splendid edifices that often boast an original combination

On the left-hand page: the majestic gothic tower of the Town Hall.
On this page: some interiors.

of architectural styles (Gothic, Renaissance, baroque), the result of reconstruction over the years.

Turning left at the House of the Black Virgin, a cubist edifice built in 1911, we enter Ovochny thr., at the end of which, to the left, is the 18th century General States Theater, dedicated to Mozart, and to the right the Karolinum, the heart of the university, founded by Charles IV in the 14th century. The only thing still remaining from the original complex, which was begun in 1348 and includes the faculties of art, law, medicine and theology, are an elegant Gothic-style bow window and the arcades on the ground floor. The present-day building is dominated by baroque style work done in the first half of the 18th century by the architect Kanka. From the very beginning, the university, which was to represent not only Bohemia, but all nations in the empire of Charles IV, was divided into Czech and German sections, both academically and in terms of student body. When, beginning in the early 15th century, Jan Hus began to spread his reformist thoughts from the university benches, the German faction strongly criticized him. Despite this, and due to the intervention of Wenceslas IV, who at first approved of his ideas, in 1409 Hus became rector of the university. His election provoked sharp protests from many German instructors and scholars, who decided to leave Prague and then founded the University of Leipzig. Faithful to the Hussite faith even after Hus was executed, after the defeat of Czech rebels at the battle of White Mountain, the university was first closed and then immediately reopened, this time under the direction of the very Catholic Jesuits. At the end of the 18th century, the university's "conversion" was accomplished through complete submission to the State. Finally, around the end of the next century, it was decided to divide the university into two branches, German and Czech. With the birth of the Czechoslovakian Republic in

1918, the university reassumed its original name of Karlova Univerzita. Leaving Zelezná Street to the right, we continue toward the very old church of St. Gallus, founded in 1232, rebuilt a century later and then radically changed by architects Carlo Lurago and Domenico Orsi in the first half of the 18th century. From the church, which stands in the center of an ancient, very lively quarter, we proceed toward the House at the Two Golden Bears, which has a magnificent Renaissance gate (1580) decorated with the sculpted figures of two bears, and elegant raceme decorations. From here, turning right, we go back up toward Malé Náměstí (Little Square), with its center adorned with an elegant 16th century well, overlooked by the Rott House, with a facade adorned with paintings and graffiti decoration. Also known as the House at the Three White Roses, in the 15th century it housed the press where the first Bible in the Czech language was printed.

From the square, we go left along the Karlova (Charles Street), opened in the 12th century, with some of the most beautiful Gothic and Renaissance houses in Prague, including the early 18th century House at the Golden Well, with its facade adorned with stucco statues of the Virgin and saints, and the House at the Golden Serpent, where the city's first café was opened in 1714.

Following the street a short way, and turning left onto Husova Street, we see the old church of St. Gallus, with its elegant baroque interior. On the right we then come to the Bethlehem Chapel (Betlémská Kaple), a modern reconstruction (1950-1952) of the original edifice built between 1391 and 1394, where Jan Hus preached. From here, coming to the nearby Náprstek Ethnographic Museum, we turn right on Liliová and then left onto Anenská. Going past the St. Anne convent, we come to the

The motto "Praga caput regni" on the Old Town's Town Hall and the wedding hall window.

Smetana Museum on the banks of the Moldau, dedicated to the famous musician.

Turning back, we return to Charles Street and come out on the Knights of the Cross square, right in front of the Charles Bridge tower, dominated by the enormous Clementinum complex, the ancient Jesuit stronghold built between the end of the 16th century and 1748, on the site of an earlier Dominican convent. Second in size only to the castle complex, it is now the site of the enormous National Library, whose fine halls hold over 4 million books.

Again following the Karlova towards Old Town, and turning left after a short distance, we come to the Mariánské Náměstí, where the imposing Clam Gallas palace stands on the

Clementinum.
Below: the baroque hall of the National Library.

corner of Husova. Built in baroque style in the early 18th century, it was based on a project by the Viennese architect Johann Bernhard Fischer von Erlach. With its characteristic neoclassical facade with the original baroque gate (1714, Matthias Braun), flanked by pairs of monumental statues of Hercules, the interior, with its sumptuous grand staircase, has splendid period decorations and frescoes. Not far from the palace, we once again come to the Old Town Square, where we can begin our visit of the city's ancient Jewish quarter.

View of the Old Town Square from the Town Hall Tower.

On this page and on the two following pages: pictures and details of St. Nicholas Church overlooking the northern side of the Old Town.

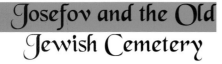

A presence in Prague since the second half of the 10th century, the Jewish community settled first at the foot of the hill, then, around the end of the 11th century, along Vysehrad Street, south of Old Town, and finally, beginning in the 12th century, near the present-day Josefov area. With its ancient traditions, the old Prague ghetto was one of the first to appear in Central Europe, and it quickly became of primary importance to the various Bohemian Jewish communities. Not unlike other Jewish communities scattered throughout Europe, despite its considerable importance to the economic life of the city, the Prague ghetto was from the very beginning rocked by pogroms (violent popular uprisings against the Jews), and seems to have been often used as a scapegoat for popular discontent. To further aggravate the situation, in 1215 the 4th Lateran Ecumenical Council promulgated severe interdictions against the Jews (including barring them from holding office, requiring them to wear a uniform, and isolating them in the ghetto), while in 1236, extending the concept of church-sanctioned, spiritual Jewish slavery to the juridical area, they were declared servants of the emperor. Despite sporadic intervention in their favor by a few rulers (especially Ottokar II, who in 1254 granted Jews a number of important rights, including the freedom of religion, administration and justice, and Rudolf II in the late 16th century), the community in the Prague ghetto was for centuries subject to discrimination, confiscation and violence. This culminated in the bloody pogrom of 1389, when Prague citizens revolted against the Jews, who were falsely accused of having poisoned the waters of the city and spreading the plague, and caused the death of over 3000 persons. The enlightened absolutism of Joseph II of Hapsburg, who came to the throne in 1780 and reigned until 1790, signaled the recognition of all civil rights for the Bohemian Jewish community, and also granted them the power to freely participate in the country's economic and cultural life, although it denied them full equality with other citizens until 1867. To crown this important historical moment, the decree on freedom of religion, which Joseph II had promulgated in 1781, was extended to Jews in 1782.

As a result of these fundamental victories, by the following century the more well-to-do Jews of Prague had the chance to live outside the walls of the ghetto, which in the meantime had been renamed Josefov in honor of Joseph II and had became the city's fifth quarter. In part abandoned by the Jews, the ghetto's houses were gradually occupied by the city's poor people of very modest means and various religious faiths, who found shelter in this quarter. The absurdities of history had forced it to grow in a rigidly limited space, and quite soon it had become inadequate and unhealthy, with its narrow streets, buildings crowded against each other, unwholesome courtyards and dark corners. For health and sanitary reasons, city administration thus decided to demolish the old ghetto, and between 1893 and the early 20th century it razed almost all of its buildings to the ground. The only thing that remained of the Josefov, the quarter so marvelously described in its most authentic and human aspects by Gustav Meyrink in *Golem*, were a few synagogues, the Jewish Town Hall and the cemetery, which was later included in the city's new zoning scheme.

Of the six synagogues that were saved from the destruction of the ghetto, the oldest and most famous is certainly Staronová Synagóga, whose rabbis included the famous

On the facing page: the Old-New Synagogue and the Jewish Town Hall.

On the facing page: "Hall of Ceremonies" building. Inside: the Jewish Museum.

Above: view of the Jewish Palace in Maiselova Street.

Rabbi Löw (1520-1609), the legendary creator of the mythical Golem. Built between 1270 and 1275, due to its isolated position away from other buildings, it remained almost completely intact until the end of the 19th century, when it underwent radical remodeling that nevertheless did not change its elegant Gothic style and the spare lines of the interior. The High Synagogue and the Pinkas Synagogue (Vyoká Synagóga and Pinkasova Synagóga) date back to the 16th century. The interior walls of the latter, built in 1535 in high Gothic style and remodeled in the first half of the following century, bear the names and dates of birth and death of about 80,000 Jews originally from Bohemia and Moravia, who were deported and killed in Nazi death camps. The edifice also has a poignant display of drawings done by Jewish children in the Nazi concentration camp at Terezín. About sixty kilometers from Prague, the camp acted as a transit station for Jews in the region, who were then transferred to death camps. Over 15,000 children passed through Terezín. Near the Pinkas Synagogue is the Maiselova Synagogue, named after the famous rabbi Mordechai Maisel, who represented the Jewish community during the era of Rudolf II, who built the synagogue in 1591. It was destroyed in the terrible 1689 fire that devastated Old Town, but was rebuilt between the 19th and 20th centuries and is now the site of an exhibit on the history of Bohemian and Moravian Jews from the 14th to the 18th centuries. The deconsecrated Klaus Synagogue, which was built in the late 17th century, has an interesting permanent exhibit dedicated to Jewish traditions and rituals.

The building stands near the entrance to the old Jewish cemetery, one of the loveliest places in not only the ghetto, but the entire city. Dating back to the first half of the 15th century, until 1787 the cemetery contin-

Pictures and details of the Old Jewish Cemetery with its 12.000 sepulchral stones.

ued to be used to bury the dead of the Jewish community, in an extremely small area within the already small ghetto. Very quickly, the modest space available became insufficient to hold new tombs. Because the Jewish religion bans the desecration of tombs, the old tombs could not be moved elsewhere, and the only solution was to place the coffins on top of each other in layers, stacking up the relative tombstones. A narrow path shaded by tall elder trees leads us through this moving place of memories, running through a sort of forest of stone markers on which, according to Jewish custom, many people still place notes with short personal messages weighted down with a small stone.

Of the 12,000 gravestones catalogued so far, we can see those of rabbis Löw and Mordechai Maisel (1528-1601).

Built in the second half of the 18th century, the Jewish Town Hall, the last survivor of the demolition of the ghetto, has a unique clock on the tower, with Hebraic numerals and hands that move counterclockwise, i.e. from right to left, like Hebraic script.

Prague Castle

Above: detail of a statue of King Charles IV.
On the right-hand page: the Castle.

Prague Castle is in reality a gigantic architectural complex, almost a city within a city, which developed over the course of the centuries on a hill above Malá Strana, or Lesser Town, which extends to the bank of the Moldau across from Staré Město, Old Town. Around the end of the 9th century, Borivoj, the first Przemyslid prince, built a castle on the hill. Shortly thereafter, he built within its walls a stone church dedicated to the Virgin, of which only a few traces remain today. In 905, again within the fortress, Vratislav I built the St. George basilica, one of the oldest Romanesque monuments in the city. It was later joined by a convent that soon became one of the principal religious and cultural centers of Prague. Twenty years later, Wenceslas, the prince of Bohemia, built the St. Vitus rotunda right in the center of the castle. After the death of Wenceslas, who was assassinated by his brother Boleslav in 935 and later canonized, the remains of the princely saint were buried in this nucleus of the present-day cathedral, in a chapel that was later expanded to a Romanesque basilica between 1060 and 1074. Having been named an episcopal seat in 973, Prague chose St. Vitus as its cathedral. In 1085, when Vratislav II, the first king of Bohemia, was crowned, the Hradcany included edifices that symbolized both temporal and spiritual power: the castle (which had been rebuilt in the meantime) and the basilica of St. Vitus. Nevertheless, in 1306, with the death of Wenceslas III, who had been assassinated just one year after he was crowned, the Przemyslid dynasty died out and the castle was abandoned until the end of the reign of John of Luxembourg. Ascending the throne in 1346, John's son Charles IV began construction on a castle that in 1355, the year in which the king of Bohemia was crowned emperor of the Holy Roman Empire, restored the hill to its full role as the country's political and religious center. In the meantime, on

November 21, 1344, Charles IV had begun work on the new St. Vitus Cathedral, which was not completed for another six centuries. Beginning in 1378, the year in which the son of Charles IV was proclaimed king under the name of Wenceslas IV, the newly reconstructed castle was abandoned for a palace in the Old Town, and only in 1484, after the bloody Hussite wars that saw it fall first into the hands of the Catholics and then to the Hussites, did it once again act as a royal residence, under the reign of Wladyslaw II Jagiello.

During the long Hapsburg period (especially under Rudolf II, who reigned from 1576 to 1611, and Maria Theresa, 1740-1780), the castle underwent profound changes, with the reconstruction of the oldest portions, the addition of new buildings, the creation of gardens, the construction of the Matthias Gate (1614), which marked its final boundaries, and most importantly, the building of the great imperial palace, with a radical transformation of the edifices that overlooked the second courtyard, as well as some of those overlooking the third.

In a position dominating the city, the imposing Viennese rococo style palace was built by Nicola Pacassi, who harmoniously combined several preexisting buildings on the site by connecting them to a new central edifice. The palace is preceded by a wide courtyard, where every day at noon the picturesque changing of the guard takes place. The wrought iron railing that encloses it in the front is surmounted by the imperial coat of arms of Maria Theresa in the center, and is interspersed with eight pillars on which stand gigantic replicas of the *Gigantomachia* sculpted by Ignaz Platzer in 1768. In the center of the palace's main face is the Matthias Gate, built by the Italian Scamozzi, which leads to the palace's

The Imperial Palace. View of the Castle with changing of the guard.

second courtyard, surrounded by edifices built during the time of Rudolf II of Hapsburg, and later unified by Pacassi. One of the most elegant, opulent areas of the sumptuous interior is the Spanish Hall and the Rudolf Gallery. In the ancient Imperial Stables (on the northern and western sides) is the Castle Gallery, which holds precious Renaissance and baroque works that belonged to the Hapsburg ruler. The Castle's third courtyard is dominated by the magnificent St. Vitus Cathedral, the quintessential symbol of the history of Prague. Built on the Romanesque basilica constructed in the second half of the 9th century on the St. Vitus rotunda and the chapel of the princely Saint Wenceslas, it was begun in 1344 during the reign of Charles IV, who appointed the French Mathieu d'Arras to build it. After he died, the appointment was passed on to Peter Parler, the famous German Gothic architect, who gave the edifice his unmistakable mark. Followed by his sons, construction work had to be interrupted due to the outbreak of the Hussite wars, which bloodied the country from 1419 to 1435. A quintessential symbol of Catholicism, in 1421 the cathedral, like the castle, was occupied by Hussite rebels. Because the enormous sums of money necessary to continue construction were lacking, except for several important sections, like the royal mausoleum (Alexandre Collin de Malines, 1566-1589), this interruption lasted for centuries.

Work did not begin again until after 1860, with the construction of the nave and the western facade and two large spires, and was completed in 1929, when the cathedral was finally consecrated, almost a thousand years after St. Wenceslas' death.

Internal courtyard of the Castle.
In the small picture: detail of the entrance;
Matthias Gate.

Only in the 1920's did the neo-Gothic western facade, decorated with a large rose window with scenes of the Creation, and its three bronze gates, replace the south side, with its splendid Golden Gate, as the main facade. The Golden Gate, adorned with a splendid mosaic on a red and gold background depicting the Last Judgment (second half of the 14th century), was designed by Parler, as was the tower that overlooks it, in Renaissance style but crowned by a baroque cupola added by Nicola Pacassi in the late 18th century.

The splendor of the interior, with a nave and two aisles with a transept, choir and side chapels, is, if possible, even further enhanced by the marvelous Gothic vault with star-shaped ribs, designed and built by Peter Parler, a true masterpiece of geometry and refinement. The 14th century triforium in the upper part of the cathedral is equally precious, and is adorned with sculpted busts of famous persons in Prague's ancient history; these are some of the most beautiful works of Czech Gothic art in the world.

On both sides of the main entrance (the west face) are three neo-Gothic chapels built in the early 20th century, as well as the splendid windows that adorn them, precious examples of Czech Art Nouveau style.

Going past the new sacristy and the 18th century organ in the cathedral to the left of the nave, is the main altar (1870), adorned by splendid wood panels, some of which were made in the 17th century, and preceded by the 16th century royal mausoleum. To the left of the altar is an elegant 17th century pulpit, while to the right is the sumptuous tomb of St. John of Nepomuk, made entirely of silver in the first half of the 18th century. Going past this monument along the right aisle, we come to the 15th century royal oratory, a splendid example of high Gothic style, with the vault decorated by a com-

St. Vitus Cathedral: view of the facade and detail of the interior.

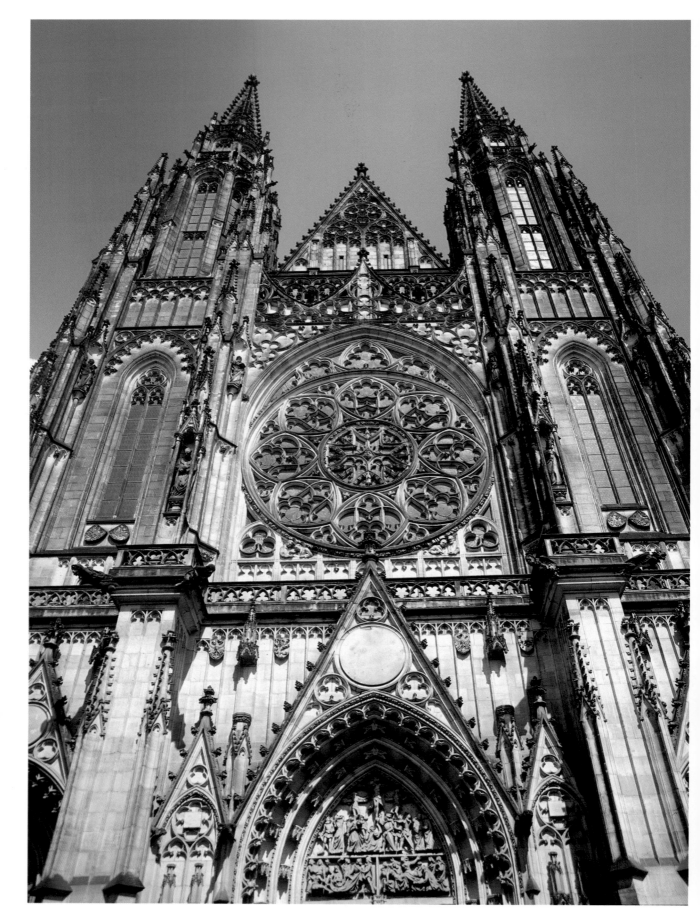

St. Vitus Cathedral: details of the facade; on pages 56-57: details of the interior.

On pages 58-59: the Golden Lane.

plicated pattern of branches and connected to the nearby royal palace by a covered passageway.

Immediately following is the Chapel of the Holy Rood, within which are stairs that descend to the royal crypt, where, in addition to the tombs of Charles IV, his son Wenceslas IV, Rudolf II and other members of the royal family, are the remains of the original St. Vitus rotunda and the Romanesque basilica. Coming out of the crypt opposite the choir, and turning to the immediate right, we come to the cathedral's greatest masterpiece, the St. Wenceslas Chapel.

Dedicated to the princely saint who was assassinated by his brother Boleslav right in the St. Vitus Chapel in 935, it was built by Peter Parler between 1362 and 1367, in pure Gothic style. The walls, completely covered with precious gems and gold decoration, are, if possible, rendered even more opulent by the 16th century frescoes that cover it, depicting episodes in the life of the saint (whose tomb is under the altar) on the upper register, and episodes from the life of Christ on the lower register.

A visit to the Castle and its treasures is not complete without a walk along the famous Golden Lane (Zlatá Ulicka), with its tiny houses built up against the castle's outer walls. According to legend, this was the street of the alchemists and magicians.

Schwarzenberg Palace

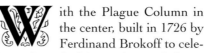

With the Plague Column in the center, built in 1726 by Ferdinand Brokoff to celebrate the end of the epidemic of plague that scourged the city in 1679, Hradčanské Náměstí, the Castle Square, is surrounded by splendid palaces that crown the majestic complex formed by the castle, the St. Vitus Cathedral and the other buildings of Prasky Hrad. With its magnificent, elegant architecture, Schwarzenberg Palace is one of the most perfect expressions of Czech Renaissance style in Prague. Jan of Lobkowitz commissioned construction of the edifice to the Italian architect Agostino Galli, who built it between 1545 and 1563, inspired by both the purest form of Italian Renaissance art and the fundamental architectural principles typical of Nordic countries. The result is a triumphant, original combination of majestic, refined elements, where the decoration blends smoothly and harmoniously with the imposing structure. The result set a fashion in Prague, and especially in the 19th century, many architects copied the style in numerous edifices and palaces in the city, although not always with the same originality.

Imported from Italy and quickly adopted by Bohemian architects, the graffito technique used to decorate the palace facade allowed Galli to lighten the massive structure of the edifice, at the same time making it more elegant. Here graffiti, restored in the 19th century by Josef Schulz, were masterfully used to reproduce the diamond-pointed ashlar work (the stone face used, for example in the Palazzo Strozzi in Florence) without rough-hewing the stone; the splendid optical illusion of the rocks protruding out from the walls vanishes gradually as we approach the palace and discover the perfect play of lines and chiaroscuro that creates the effect of relief ashlar work on the smooth walls.

While we have noted that the lower part of the palace is clearly inspired

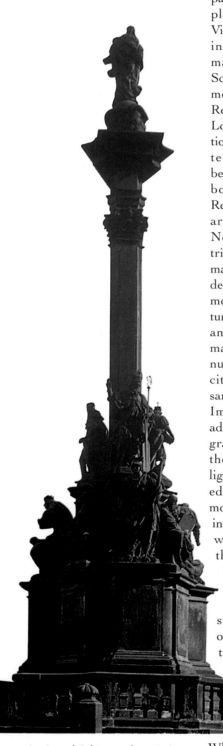

Panoramic view of Schwarzenberg Palace, a typical Renaissance Palace.

by Italian Renaissance architecture, in particular Florentine architecture, the upper portion, dominated by Gothic pediments on three levels, displays a typically Nordic structural style. Characteristic of Bohemian architecture, the Gothic pediments are here formed by three superimposed levels articulated by engaged columns and dotted with extremely linear, light trabeation, with the end (and the top of the Gothic pediment) decorated by urns.

Originally owned by the Lobkowitz family, one of the most prominent in the city, the palace was purchased by the Schwarzenberg family in the early 18th century, and since 1945

has been home to the Prague Military History Museum (Historická Expoice, Vojenské Muzeum). In the various halls decorated with splendid frescoes on the ceilings, we can admire numerous historical paintings (including an interesting 1859 Battle of Solferino from the Austrian school), as well as precious collections of weapons and uniforms used by the troops that fought in the many wars over the long period from the Slavic era to the First World War. Of significant interest is the section explaining the military strategies and tactics used by Hussite forces over the course of history.

The palace, whose complete name is actually Schwarzenberg Lobkowitz, in memory of its purchasers and first owners, is flanked by another edifice, the former Schwarzenberg Palace. Of no artistic or architectural interest, it was built in 1776 and 1861 in Empire style by the architect Frantisek Pavícek, and is currently the home of the Swiss Confederation embassy.

Pictures and details of Schwarzenberg Palace.

Episcopal Palace and Hradčanské Náměstí Area

The lower portion of Hradčanské Náměstí, to the left of the Castle, overlooks the majestic, extremely elegant palace with its white facade, which is still the site of the Prague archbishopric. It was built in the year immediately following the great fire that on June 2, 1541 first caused severe damage to Malá Strana (Lesser Town, located at the foot of the hill) and then rose as far as the castle, devastating Hrad and the surrounding area. With earlier buildings swept away, the Prague nobility and church immediately took over the now vacant area and erected important buildings and palaces in the shadow of the castle. The palace was built in 1562-1564 by Ulrico Aostalli, based on a design by the architect Bonifaz Wohlmut, but as early as 1675 and 1694 it was restructured and to some extent remodeled by Jean-Baptiste Mathey. Finally, during the first half of the 18th century, archbishop Antonín Prichowsky commissioned the architect Johann Josef Wirch to redo the facade, which had originally been in neo-Renaissance style. Linear and elegant, the current facade, on three levels dotted with pilasters and engaged columns, has interesting rococo style elements, in particular the balconies and bull's eye windows on the second floor. The main building, flanked by two slightly projecting side wings, opens out to the ground floor from a beautiful gate, probably the work of Jean-Baptiste Mathey, surmounted by the coat of arms of the Prague archbishopric.

In Prague, which Charles IV named an archbishopric in 1344, the palace immediately became an important political and religious symbol. As early as 1562, in fact, Ferdinand I of Hapsburg, who ascended the throne in 1526, purchased it for the private residence of the Catholic bishop, thus celebrating the return of the Roman Catholic faith to Prague after the bloody period of the Hussite wars (1419-1435) and the final defeat of the heresy of Jan Hus. A century later, after the Battle of White Mountain in 1620, which marked a victory for the Catholic troops of Ferdinand II of Hapsburg over Czech rebels who had proclaimed the Calvinist Frederick V as king, the symbolic force of the grandiose episcopal palace once again proclaimed Bohemia's return to Hapsburg domination and Catholic predominance.

A small road to the left of the episcopal palace leads to Sternberskí Palác, an edifice built in a number of stages between the late 17th century and early 18th century by great baroque artists of the period such as Domenico Martinelli and the Dientzenhofers, who created baroque masterpieces in Prague like the church of St. Nicholas in the Old Town and the church of St. John Nepomuk on the Rocks, and another Italian, Giovanni Battista Alliprandi. Facing a beautiful palace garden, the elliptical pavilion houses precious collections of old European art in the Prague National Gallery (Národmí Galerie v Praze). The Gallery originated in the late 18th century, when, in order to create a public picture gallery in the style of those found in the great capitals of the period, Count Franz Josef Sternberg founded the Czech society of the Friends of Art in Bohemia. Numerous representatives of the nobility and rich Czech burghers immediately joined the project by making large donations, and by the end of the 19th century, the picture gallery already had a wealth of masterpieces by celebrated artists from all over Europe, including Italy (with a splendid collection of works from the 16th and 17th centuries) France and Spain, the Netherlands and Germany (with, respectively, Pieter Breugel the Elder's *Haymaking* and Rembrandt's *The Old Scholar* and the *Madonna of the Rosary* by Albrecht Dürer in 1506, the most valuable work in the museum), and, of course, Bohemia. After the 1918 armistice, with the birth of the independent Republic and the alliance that Edvard Benesz entered into with the Soviet Union in

The Episcopal Palace, detail with view of the St. Vitus Cathedral. Above: the coat of arms on the facade.

1935, which signaled Czechoslovakia's passage under Soviet influence, the picture gallery was purchased by the state and in 1945 was incorporated into the Prague National Gallery. From February 1948, with the ascent of the communists to power and the beginning of the process of Stalinization, numerous works of art were confiscated from private parties and transferred to the Gallery. After a law was promulgated in 1990 requiring artistic and other assets that had been taken during the communist period to be returned to their rightful owners, some of the works that were added to the Gallery in this manner had to be returned to their original owners. Previously held here, the collections of modern art, including other masterpieces of French art and the important group of cubist works donated to the Gallery by the collector Vincenc Kramár, were recently transferred to the Museum of Modern and Contemporary Art at the Veletrzní Palace, which along with the Prague Capital City Gallery (at the Troja Castle) and the St. Agnes convent (with its collection of 19th century Czech paintings and sculpture) offers a detailed look at the evolution of art during this historic period.

The Episcopal Palace.

The Loreto Sanctuary

Founded by the princess Benigna Katerina Lobkowitz in the early 17th century, the sanctuary is one of the principal architectural complexes and churches in the city. The various buildings that comprise it are arranged around the Holy House, a replica of the home of the Virgin Mary, who according to legend was flown by angels from Nazareth to Loreto, Italy, in the 13th century. The heart and largest building of the complex was built by Giovanni Domenico Orsi between 1621 and 1631, the day after the Battle of White Mountain, and was immediately hailed as a symbol of the victory of Catholicism over the Protestant Hussites. The facade, interspersed with sixteen Corinthian columns, is decorated by relief work depicting episodes in the life of the Virgin Mary, and the interior holds a precious silver altar consecrated to Mary. Over subsequent years, the cloister with its fine frescoes, and other sanctuary monuments, were built around the Holy House. The facade, begun in 1721 by Christoph Dientzenhofer and completed by his son in 1723, is adorned with sculptures on the theme of the Annunciation. The bulb-shaped bell tower in the central building holds the famous carillon by Peter Naumann (1694), and plays a different aria each hour. The baroque Church of the Nativity, the largest in the complex, holds precious frescoes, including the one in the choir, the *Presentation to the Temple* by W.L. Reiner. The sanctuary's treasury holds jewels and precious objects that belonged to Prague nobility.

The Loreto Sanctuary.

The Charles Bridge

A pedestrian zone since 1974, the bridge (516 m long and 10 m wide, resting on sixteen piers) crosses the Moldau and the small island of Kampa, connecting Staré Město, Old Town, to Malá Strana, or Lesser Town, at the foot of the Castle hill. In 1357, Charles IV commissioned it to Peter Parler, the architect who built St. Vitus Cathedral, to replace the Judith Bridge, the city's first stone bridge, which was destroyed when the river flooded in 1342.

The street level, decorated by numerous groups of statues that have made the bridge famous throughout the world, winds through two imposing gates. One faces Old Town and the other Lesser Town, and both are in Gothic style, although they were built during different periods. The first, designed by Parler himself and erected at the same time as the bridge, is a solid, massive tower 40 m high, built primarily for defensive purposes and decorated on the outside by fine sculptures, including the celebratory portraits of Charles IV, Wenceslas IV and St. Vitus. Inside, the beautiful Gallery on the first floor offers a splendid view of the bridge and city. The second gate was built in the early 15th century near the only tower of the Judith Bridge that was still standing. Only fifty years later, another tower was built to accompany it, similar to but more linear than the one Parler had designed on the opposite side of the bridge.

Between the 18th and the 19th centuries, other statues were added to the monuments that decorated the bridge when it was first built - the Crucifixion, St. John of Nepomuk and the Pietá. Today, for purposes of preservation and security, almost all of these statues have been replaced by replicas (the originals are in the epi-

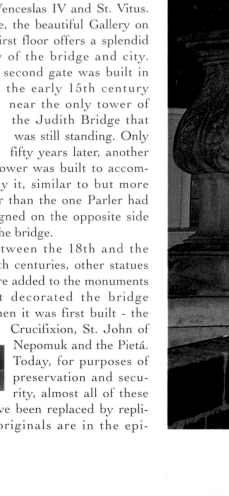

Above: statue of the Charles Bridge; on the right: nocturnal view.

The Bridge, in the smaller pictures a detail of the Tower towards the Old Town.

graphic section of the National Museum).

Starting from the tower in Old Town, the first sculptures on the right are the group with the Madonna and St. Bernard and the Madonna with St. Dominick and St. Thomas Aquinas (18th century). These are followed by the Crucifixion, done around 1630 to replace the previous sculpture, destroyed during the Hussite wars. Statues of saints precede and follow the oldest (1683) and most famous monument on the bridge, the St. John Nepomuk, in bronze, which depicts the martyrdom of the saint, one of the most venerated in Prague, as he is thrown into the waters of the Moldau in 1393 by order of Wenceslas IV.

Going back down the bridge from the Lesser Town gate, on the opposite side we can admire the statue of St. Wenceslas and the "Turk on the Bridge" group (18th century), depicting saints John of Matha and Felix as they free Christians imprisoned by the infidels. Following are the statue of the bishop St. Adalbert and the splendid group with the mystical vision of St. Lutgarda (1710).

Passing the stairs that descend to the island of Kampa, of note are the statue of St. Nicholas of Tolentino, the group with saints Vincent Ferrer and Procopius (behind it is a replica of a statue of a 16th century knight) and St. Francis Xavier, with the self-portrait of the sculptor Brokoff to the left of the saint.

On these two pages: views of the Charles Bridge.

On the two following pages: on the left, the St. Vitus Cathedral seen from the Charles Bridge. Above: Charles Bridge. Below: street artists and a statue on the bridge.

Above: equestrian statue in Wenceslas Square. On the right-hand page: Wenceslas Square.

After rebuilding the palace within the castle walls, obtaining the Pope's recognition of Prague as the episcopal seat, and in 1344 beginning construction on the St. Vitus Cathedral, in 1346 Charles (born of the marriage between John of Luxembourg, the king of Bohemia, and Elizabeth, daughter of the last Przemyslid king, Wenceslas III), not yet crowned Charles IV, decreed the foundation of Nové Město, New Town. Originator of a profound urban transformation (which included, among other things, construction of the Charles Bridge beginning in 1357, which connected Staré Město, Old Town, to Malá Strana, or Lesser Town, at the foot of the Castle hill) that radically changed the face of Prague, transforming it into one of the greatest cities in Europe by the end of his reign, Charles IV thus intended to allow the city to further expand beyond the limited and now inadequate area of Staré Město, Old Town. Through his foundation decree of April 3, 1347, he thus ordered the quarters that had gradually developed outside the Old Town, the heart of the aristocracy, the bourgeoisie and the economic life of the city, to be incorporated within New Town, which quickly became the center of various handicrafts and commercial activities that gave Prague a new, strong impetus.

With large streets and broad avenues, New Town also had three vast cross-shaped areas that were connected by cross streets that were entirely used for livestock, horse and hay markets. Of the three areas, which respectively became the Karlovo, Václavské and Senovazné Náměstí, the second is beyond doubt the most important, famous, and largest square of Nové Město. Wenceslas Square, which was so renamed during the revolution of 1848, has over time continued to act as a quintessential symbol of Czech national identity and the spirit of resistance of the city's inhabitants; this was reiterated not only during the Prague Spring of 1968, when

Prague residents gathered to try to stop Soviet tanks, but in the late 1980's as well, during the "Velvet Revolution," when it acted as a stage for the popular proclamation of former dissident Václav Hável as President of the Republic. On this and on numerous other occasions, the enormous square (50 x 60 meters in size) attracted immense crowds gathered in the name of liberty, which had been denied to the city for too long and in too many ways. The square has seen demonstrations, struggles, and protests, often in the form of enormous yet peaceful gatherings; this too is where the young philosophy student Jan Palach sacrificed his life by dousing himself with gasoline and setting himself ablaze. As a symbol of this unquenchable thirst for freedom and justice, on one side of Václavské Náměstí is an equestrian statue of St. Wenceslas and the four patron saints of Bohemia, and on the other the moving monument to the victims of communism, a simple cushion of flowers and candles on which Prague residents place the photographs of those who paid for liberty with their lives.

View of Wenceslas Square and the National Museum.

Demolished in the 1870's, as was the New Town fortress of which it was a part, the Horse Gate, which stood on the far south end of the square, was replaced by the majestic, neo-Renaissance National Museum (Národní Muzeum) between 1885 and 1890. Founded in 1818 by Czech patriots who had played a leading role in the national rebirth, the museum, with a sumptuous marble interior that houses anthropology, natural history, mineralogy and archaeology exhibits, also holds a magnificent library that is famous for its medieval codices.

Along the two sides of the square, which is always extremely crowded, next to shops, cafés and restaurants, are splendid palaces that, along with neighboring areas, constitute a true open air architectural museum, testimony to the continued vivacity of Prague architecture. While the elegant house of the architect Antonín Wiehl, decorated with frescoes and graffiti on the facade, is neo-Renaissance, the Hotel Evropa, built in 1903-1906, with its superb Art Nouveau decorations, is the best example of Secession style in Prague. On the side of the square opposite the National Museum, the Koruna Palace, so called due to the crown that surmounts its turret, is done in a "Babylonian" style that

On these two pages and on the two following pages: the National Theater.

expresses the interest in archaeological research in Mesopotamia underway during the late 19th and early 20th centuries. On the opposite side, no. 12, the Peterka House, a work by Jan Kotera, is a prime example of geometric Art Nouveau architecture. Behind the square is the interesting Muzeum Mucha, dedicated to the great Prague Art Nouveau painter Alfons Mucha (1860-1939).

From Václacské Náměstí, proceeding toward the Moldau along the pedestrian area Na Príkope, an authentic open air museum of Prague architecture, we come to another important edifice in New Town, the National Theater (Národní Divadlo), a symbol of Czech artistic history. In the late 18th century, at the time of a resurgence of national pride, and inspired and nourished by the Enlightenment, the Czech people felt the need to found a theater that would become a temple of the country's national culture. The decision to build the theater was made as early as 1849, but lacking funds, which the Austrian administration refused to provide, only in May 1868 was it possible to begin construction, using the enormous sums of money collected through a popular subscription initiated in Bohemia and Moravia. The construction of the opera house, which the people saluted with true joy, was commissioned to Josef Zítek, one of the most famous architects of the time. The dream of those who had generously contributed to construction of the theater was, however, shattered in the summer of 1881, when just a few weeks after Zítek's neo-Renaissance edifice was opened, it was completely destroyed by fire. It was immediately decided to rebuild it, this time as well financed with voluntary contributions from the people, and it was built in only two years based on a project by Josef Schulz, who designed the National Museum.

The main facade of the theater, which has a number of levels, is decorated by an elegant loggia with five arches surmounted by a terrace with statues of Apollo and the Muses on the balustrade. The two side wings are crowned by bronzes with the Winged Victory on a chariot. The imposing theater culminates in the splendid cupola with a blue roof dotted with stars. Inside, adorned by a profusion of decorations (like those on the outside, by leading Czech artists of the late 19th and early 20th centuries), the most spectacular room is certainly the sumptuous concert hall with its luxurious royal box, the three orders of boxes, the bal-

On the left-hand page: The New Town Hall.

On the two following pages: Kranner Fountain and Hanavsky Pavilion.

On this page: the Culture Palace.
On the right-hand page: the Forum Hotel.

cony and the gallery overlooking the stage, hidden by an elegant curtain on which Vojtech Hynais used red and gold to depict the collection of funds from the people necessary to build the theater.

The hall is crowned by an elegant frescoed ceiling with the allegorical figures of the Arts.

Between 1970 and 1980, the theater underwent major restoration that

involved construction of the New Stage, a new wing complete with concert hall and services (restaurant and coffee bar) done in glass by Karel Prager. In November 1983, when the theater was reopened following restoration, Smetana's *Libuse* was performed in the concert hall, the same work that had opened the Czech National Theater a hundred years earlier.

INDEX

Distributed by:
STONE BRIDGE s.r.o.
Křížovnické náměstí 2 - PRAHA
Tel. +420.2.2409 - 7483 Fax: +420.2.2409. - 7484
E-mail: sbridge@czn.cz